Pink purse girl

Pink purse girl

Susan L. Helwig

Wolsak and Wynn

© Susan Helwig, 2006

No part of this publication may be reproduced, stored in a retrieval system or transmitted, in any form or by any means, without the prior written consent of the publisher or a licence from The Canadian Copyright Licensing Agency (Access Copyright). For an Access Copyright licence, visit www.accesscopyright.ca or call toll free to 1-800-893-5777.

Cover image: Ruth Hartman, hartmanr@pathcom.com
Cover design: Rachel Rosen, rachel@fairlyunusual.com
Author's photograph: Robert Barnett of B+W Custom Photo
Typeset in Adobe Garamond, printed by The Coach House Printing Co., Toronto, Ontario

Some of these poems have appeared in *Acta Victoriana, TheAntigonish Review, Ariel, The Avatar Review, Canadian Literature, Canadian Woman Studies, Common Sky (anthology), CV2, The Dalhousie Review, Descant, Grain,* and the *Hart House Review.*

The publishers gratefully acknowledge the support of the Canada Council for the Arts, the Ontario Arts Council, and the Book Publishing Industry Development Program (BPIDIP) for their financial assistance.

Wolsak and Wynn Publishers Ltd
69 Hughson Street North, Suite 102
Hamilton, Ontario, Canada L8R 1G5
www.wolsakandwynn.ca

Library and Archives Canada Cataloguing in Publication
Hellwig, Susan L., 1950-
    Pink purse girl / Susan Helwig.

Poems.
ISBN 1-894987-14-4

I.   Title.

PS8565.E464P66   C811'.6   C2006-904273-X

For Malca

Contents

If I were a ravenous bee   11
Personal ad   12
Doing it   13
About Starbucks©   14
Venus – always bragging about that…   15
The trams in Warsaw   16
Mrs. Rosen, your husband is empty of love   17
Flying over Montreal, the city at my feet   18
Another kind of wedding   19
If an eagle danced   20
His arms are so full   21
What he was doing   22
The heart is empty so far   23
Traum Papa   24
I am in Paris   25
Without protection   26
Our sorrow is bigger   27
Love songs of the 60s   28
Hunger   29
England in November   30
Five days away   31
Why I haven't written   33
I've smelled the drains in a thousand European bakeries   34
Speak, Costas!   35
Foreign vistas   36
This is where I start   37
From my corner   38
Weatherman   39
Nothing is wasted   40
Tears for my father   41

Under stand   42
My version   43
Sometimes I feel so darn catty   44
A hooker flashes her breasts on Jarvis   45
Sons: drowning   46
Medicine Man   48
Zumburger   49
Her on the walkway by the Faculty Club   50
Friend ship   51
Snow's prayer   53
How to get the gun out of the loaf   54
Ice again   55
Pentecost   56
The next attack   57
She crosses the hump-back bridge in twilight   58
Your haircut is from Africa   59
Prehistoric   60
Sunset Bar & Grill   62
Losing the poetry contest   63
Comfort, Swan, Gentles   64
Music, a food for love   66
Room for love   68
Art: he paints my portrait with gifts   69
Overcoats: hers and hers   71
That night, my first song   72
Artist's basement   73
His sister   76
Notes for a piano   77
When Dot Huffman dies   78
Before first kiss   79
I could ask   80

Resolution   81
A lesbian and her lover in Siberia   82
Once, back then   83
Workshop   84
Days of nothing   85
A good poem is better than ten novels   86
Poetry makes my living   87

If I were a ravenous bee

an eater natural-born
I would plunder these early reds
for all they're worth
call
when I was sated
call all my friends
and stretch the drunken daze
to a week or two;
when I got too tired to buzz about
I would write the story of this sticky neon fountain

if I were another kind of bee
not natural
one who only watched the scarlet dance
one who knew blood better than beauty
I would sit sidelined and wait
keen my waiting and longing
and when the carmine had long gone
borne down the creek in flash flood
I would see her pale sisters standing alone
violet ruffle
orange ice
chantilly mauve
ask each languorous one to dance
whisper *Bella* in her ear
ask her to be mine
for just one night.

Personal ad

I am not afraid of silence
when there is nothing to say
I hate men's cologne
I like to ride the streetcar
with no destination in mind
even if the driver has told me his
yes, I am married
but only out of cowardice
I still have lots of love to give when it rains

Doing it

As for my courage, it reached out its hand only that once,
when it brushed back your hair and stared at your ruby earring,
suspended.

About Starbucks©*

when You first appreciate it
the single-origin of the beans.
your smooth, cup of it
across a cup of
a blend. of it
first the sidewalks. have notes
recognize There's subtleties and tantalizing thought
when You begin to tingle
You experience something about Each day.
special and amazingly delicious.
when the very flavor
the feeling of a cup
your buds taste coffee.
Or each aroma
wafts at You under many doors

**Last summer at Starbucks, one of the baristas gave me a fridge magnet advertisement. Each word was a separate tile. I teased them apart and made them into my own poem, retaining the capitalization and punctuation of the original. It still sounds like an ad, albeit one written by a copywriter on acid.*

Venus – always bragging about that *meshuggeneh* son of hers

When I brought the boy along to watch
I had no idea where it would lead

Why, just the other day
he loosed the strings from Olga's bundles of onions
so she could find her balance, eased the cramps in her legs
and those onions in a Big Red Box on the back of her bike
you know what I'm saying

Some weeks before, he slipped a breeze into the lecture hall
so that Vera's blouse moved, just a bit, mind you
I've got a body here, she said, under these clothes
and get this, the man involved dreamed himself the Seducer!

In April, I'm dying if I'm lying
he cooked up Sadie's vegetables, all the ready ripe ones
cold from their winter storage, turnips and such
and fat spears of asparagus, this year's crop
from his whispers, she sensed the earth
apples going to ground, these she knew to bury
food for next year's doings

One last thing
you okay with this?
He got an ever-so-bashful farmer, unasked
driving Golda all the way to Flesherton
checking out that barn and silo she's always dreamed of
while her husband was away, no less.

The trams in Warsaw

After the snow the trams in Warsaw
grieve through the ghetto

Mustard
flavour of murder, charnel house, autopsy, regret

Cobalt blue
you are in love
it is brief
it is spring

Red
those dirty sheets again
salty and crushed
sometimes beads
Christmas lights
a poinsettia for your hair

Trams
and now the milkman
with all his white clinking
glass on glass, bottle on bottle
after the trams.

Mrs. Rosen, your husband is empty of love

Take the Pyrex cake pan to the library
for the dusty hours before
Prisoner of Zenda
which you will watch alone

When he nags you for a clean white shirt
tell him the only one left
is wet from your own wash hung beside

Penelope's
that's where he's going
cherry coat and red cravat will mark him
from his clutch of James Dean companions

Mrs. Rosen, your husband is empty of love.

Flying over Montreal, the city at my feet

Send me the address where you once lived
I'll stand on the sidewalk
eat a pizza in the rain

ride a bus, a people can, up from the station

if only I'd written this down in those days
before I knew about seeds
when I watched yours spill onto the quilt
never thought about acreages
farms separated by random fences
how all this could grow from that patchwork

eating pizza
my shoes off, held aloft in my other hand
feet sore from walking up such a steep hill
holes in my stockings
and that gap
just above the stocking tops
that cold bare place
where white skin is ready for your caress

let me stand
and look
pizza in one hand, shoes in the other
holes in my stockings from the concrete
rain kisses on my neck, cheek, closed eyes
pretend sleep
you will not sense me there.

Another kind of wedding

I did not see bridal veils in cherry blossoms
like Anne Shirley driving up to Green Gables
an empty basket waiting to be filled
with love-lies-bleeding
didn't need a veil to hide
modesty or the happiness of a June bride
ran right out into the field where he raged
he always got his way
he would plough through the air for me
get me what I wanted when I danced on his back
poet-friends gawking from the cherry trees
on and on we would thrust in broad daylight
elbow out the others
into the violet evening when no-one could see
so there was no point anymore
then he carried me to his small black place
took off that grey tuxedo, loosed his pearl studs
let me see his great big need
asked for love, asked for tenderness
that empty gaping thing.

If an eagle danced

If an eagle danced, he would tango
not bothering to hide his talons
yes, they are for killing
but just now, they like to feel the steps

And not ask, am I holding you too tight?
He would tango through all the rhythms of raptor love
where his body stopped and mine started, no-one could tell

He'd get me humming
Love is a many-feathered thing
and other eagle tunes

Bow at the end
Wow! An eagle bows to me!
No rush for what comes later
his nature
with gentle wing, he'd steer me to the groaning
board – red meat, wine, Gitanes, all good things
a table in the presence of
Look, how he makes me blaspheme!

His arms are so full

There is no room for me

One hand holds a Pepperette
and while I am willing to kiss him
through the foggy garlic
or even chew the dried-up stick
with such of my molars that are left
or don't cry out at the grinding
he doesn't know this
at a glance
like I do

His other arm steadies a small son on his shoulder
this is a surprise to me
a new addition
child of a second marriage, perhaps

Assuming I could make short work of the Pepperette
beside it stands his wife, not older
but robust and thick
with the promise of more love, more offspring, more

It's not enough that his arm can slip around her waist
there's also his first-born
a daughter approaching seventeen
the girl I was when we first met

And I stand here
framing the shot
out of the picture.

What he was doing

What he was doing when last I saw him:
buttoning up his shirt
both hands, fingers smoothing the buttons through
he does up his shirt in no great hurry
looks down to match each button on the right
with the buttonhole on the left
in the half-light

After some months, next spring, perhaps,
I will see him by chance
at a party, or on the subway
and when the formulas have died down, I will say

The moon the other night, did you see it? So blue and cold, just pushed its way between the black tree bones.

The heart is empty so far

I'm only twelve you know, I'll be thirteen in September, I got this bracelet from my Gran, I might paste my Dad in, he's building me a new bedroom in the basement, my Mom, well not my real Mom, my step-mom, she's having a baby soon, or maybe I'll paste in a picture of my cat, his name is Cuddie, that's short for Cuddles, I'm going to be a paediatric nurse some day, my sister, she's going to be a physiotherapist; next September, that's my birthday, I'll be taking the bus to high school, it's okay, though, because my step-brother will be on the same bus as me, he's fifteen; do you know how to play hangman? Here, I'll show you, it's really easy, see, you think of a word, and then put down the empty lines, one for every letter, and a space between the words if there's more than one, and then you draw the hangman's platform, like this, and then I try and guess your words, and every time I get a letter wrong, you draw another part of me that hangs from the rope, even my hair, that's another part you can draw, and if you get my whole body done, and my hair too, before I guess your words, or your word, if it's only one, then I hang and you win. Then it'll be my turn. Ready?

Traum Papa

In the age after cuddle and pinch
past grab and giggle
he is still your Papa

The painter with spattered overalls and a braid
auburn like your mother
love in the afternoon

A new tug with the cellist
want and need, a sad, a European moustache

Inside every one of them you will try to love
your Papa

Even in fantasies, in rhythm
rub and rub the
drawing out
it's still your Papa

In the silence, in the dark
urging you, compelling you
the rough hands, the strength
Papa again.

I am in Paris

in a hotel of mirrors
I wake in the night to show my passion
I toss my babies in the *poubelle* down the alleyway
I shop for furs at *Le Printemps*
I trade your groceries for *parfum*
to give away to my new *amie*
I phone my husband for money
while you are on your knees
tell him I am dying of love
I'll be home soon

I write all this down
in a café where I look for a new lover
and quickly turn the page when he comes over
to hand me my drink

Later I tell my therapist
I say it is the fault of mirrors and of Paris
I think he agrees
when he tries to kiss me

Without protection

She's at the frontier, a hole in her umbrella
the size of a berry

or

She approaches the border, a berry for an umbrella
small now, but it will grow

There are new clusters of berries in the country to the east.

Forty Satie umbrellas they found in his rooms when he died
he left them at home or carried them furled
played the Montmartre piano wet
If this wasn't about berries, I could stop saving those rainy days

The tightrope walker carries an umbrella
is rain really her danger or the berry carpet below?

When she wafts back to earth
the smell of berries marks the way
crushed on dry brown toast
that sweet red rain
the other side of the wire.

Our sorrow is bigger

Our sorrow is bigger, much bigger than yours
Today we build from the rubble
(I'm sure you won't mind helping)
a bigger and better monument
to those of ours who died
innocent citizens of a glorious land
we will start from here

Once you were our friends
or so we thought, that time we shook hands
at an undisclosed location

Our sorrow is greater, much greater than yours
What you feel is not sorrow, but defeat
you've been caught, found out
and like a parent, loving but tough
our leader is waiting, patiently waiting
to show you what freedom means
you, and all your family, can enjoy his protection

Our sorrow is bigger, and will last longer
Every schoolchild has learned the date, in our language
and marks it yearly with silence
poems will be written, hymns will be sung
remove your cap, bow your head, give thanks

Liberation has begun.

Love songs of the 60s

I'm singing them old lovesick words again, Mama

that word, that word

I'd walk a mile for a word
Come to where the words are, come to Love Country
Like the sea, words keep calling you back

that word, that word

Cause there's Love, and then there's Words for Love
They leave you breathless
They taste good, like a word for love should
When you're out of love, you're out of words for love

that word, that word

that spoonful.

Hunger

I rode with Zapata
always hungry then
but we could get ourselves fed
villages that hated us
there we grabbed food with our teeth
ravished the children as the three o'clock sun
glinted off our smiles
then we burned the place down

Villages that loved us, of course,
they would meet us on the road
carrying roast chickens, blood-red tomatoes,
their daughters, too, offered on a platter
the whole enchilada
no need to smile, though we often did,
just by way of thanks
sometimes burnt the place down anyway
we were so drunk and happy

These days, at the end of a dirt path
I don't see much in the way of girls and food
no teeth to flash or eat with
when Juanita came to the door last night
looking for her brother
come in, come in, I said
raised my empty arms wide
a smile of belly peeked out under my shirt
I was in love already
I rode with Zapata
– a military cloak I quickly threw on –
here, over here, the bed is soft, it cannot hurt you
your family is large?
lots of brothers and sisters?

England in November

Here darkness falls at once
perilous
no twilight
no shoulder
the road the ravine
I am dead

Here the Brave
the New
the Euro World
the cage flies open
rats at my face

There'll always be an
orange, a lemon
a Saint in the field

Tonight it's stale
in the back row
talk that could be English all around
hands slide down clammy flesh
dirty fingernails
touching myself
in middle age.

Five days away

alone
met him in the *Bois de Boulonge*
my friends all have lovers
this is what they're waiting to hear about
back home
this will be my souvenir
practice my French tongue, so to speak
took him back to my hotel
it was over fast
didn't know Parisian small talk
thought he'd never leave

then at Versailles
feeling so old, walls thinning and going dry
he was the American in shades
who asked the price of the gold horses and chariot
took me in a rental car to his hotel
the same
except I left soon after

next day in twilight outside the *Louvre*
a man walking his dog
it was the colder wind, or memories of my father
or the way the dog looked at the boats on the *Seine*
at a nearby café we drank *vin rouge*
kissed fondled   I cried
then there was the question of the dog
so we went back to his flat

in a bookstore I was taking the pulse of immortality
lunchtime – he asked for Sartre
lunchtime – he had to get back
so we went to the *Jardin des Tuileries*
just talked about doing it
that is what writers do, and I told him I was one
not believing it myself, so long since I've done anything

the last morning, I offered myself to a boy
at Jim Morrison's dewy grave
we did it standing there
didn't flinch when the *concièrge* shooed us away
impudent pigeons.

Why I haven't written

Slept so far
felt like 175 truckloads of mattresses got piled on my
jet-lagged body

first day, okay, I can understand that
but on into the week of a one-week vacation?

Thought for sure the river outside the hotel
would wake me with its
bubble and chatter
when I finally got out this morning
(Wednesday already, can you believe it?)
nothing but silence from the muddy chocolate river bed
no rain, no water, nothing wet in Europe
for several years now
or so the story goes
Did see a guy (pater familias?) watering straws
or *pailles*, as they would say here
For Heaven's sake, stop wasting water, I wanted to tell him
nothing will grow from plastic, don't you know?

There's a sun-washed passageway, off to the side
with an ersatz Bridge of Sighs
without strolling down there, I know it leads nowhere

Remember Midge who was so rude to me
last choir concert?
Saw her today walking up to apologize
(all the way to Switzerland for that!)
when she got closer, realized it was only me in a mirror

All for now.

I've smelled the drains in a thousand European bakeries

let sticky pear juice wash down my fingers
onto cobblestoned streets
wandered like a cloud of Gitanes beside the canal
sent a dozen postcards to abandoned lovers
in my head

It all comes down to
it comes down
it comes to

Speak, Costas!

Tell me that gulls circled the fishing boat, cried out, you threw
them scraps from the galley kitchen, your domain below decks,
speak so they'll know I'm not making this up, what was that story
again, the one about the hot red fruit from bursting orchards,
the way the wind blew from Africa some nights, the day the ship
docked at Napoli, the soccer star surrounded by young boys,
or on Patmos, shore leave, the beaten gold of the icons, now
I see only the grey photograph, Holy Mother of God, the fire
extinguisher, City of Toronto inspection tag, the pigeons out on
Pape, snow and ice, crumbs from the toaster, your narrow little
restaurant, *tomatts* from the steel bowl in the fridge, say these out
loud, tales of the Mediterra.

Foreign vistas

I will sit on the bed, stare at the wall
different bed, different wall
no appointments to keep, no friends to call
new eyes

I will descend to the bar, order *un verre*
different bar, different choice
new sound to my voice

Vous désirez, Madame?

Vin rouge, s'il vous plait.

And *Madame* will close her purse with a snap
a hard bright noise, a compact smile
as Signoret might have done
once in a while

Upstairs again, after *mon verre*
lounge on the bed, gaze at the wall
new sights, new eyes, new voice, that's all.

This is where I start

All night her fingers curl and uncurl
prayer or begging
He'd called at midnight with a reworked phrase, better, he said
Now in the half-light
waking from the orisons of both hands
and searching through four typed sheets, one page of notes
she cannot find a place for these words
the insertion point
where they belong
what he's given
not what she needs.

From my corner

they are looking at seeds
they are making plans
they lean together over the table
their eggs are golden
they are plotting a garden
their story is round and big
they will have children
they have lots of time
he writes perfect novels
she knits cozy cardigans
they sing modern harmonies
they will travel to France
they read the New York Times
they discuss Ondaatje
they are in love.

Weatherman

Always he would be checking
watching the sky
asking my mother, in worn-out German
what did they have for weather tonight?
if he'd missed the six o'clock news
when he plowed late in the fields
or dinner-gathered at midday
we would have to hush when the forecast came on

That was only one prophecy he listened to
there were others
the rooster scratching under a certain thorn tree
the cat munching grass
cattle who lumbered and lowed
back to the stable early, heavy with milk
or heard his own bones while they were still young
free of pain
one day's weather made all the difference
a good crop or a bad

The day he went away
he must have tuned in the noon report
out of habit, not need
he had no hay of his own lying cut, ready to harvest
then he saw a new field, just across the river
threatened by mad clouds

Took the crop that afternoon
in one quick wagonload
over and done with
for good.

Nothing is wasted

Ivory wave of breast drew you to my body
that milky curve fed our children
then cancer opened it like a blossom
gave doctors cells to clone
that godly art travelled the world
breathed life into Dolly the sheep
her lanolin smoothed a path for the Queen's tears
at the scene of the massacre
that salt water joined the rivers to the sea
where they swelled into a soft cold bed
for all the pieces from the plane
seats
parcels
legs
breasts.

Tears for my father

How can they stain?
They are only watery, as the light is in December
when I was born

Christmas that year pushed washday
to Tuesday
and you helped clean the clothes,
hang them outside to dry in the iced air

The rest of the nativity is vague
did you stand by
a dazed but supportive Joseph
while her water broke?

Did your eyes brim with love
the day you drove us home from the hospital?

More to the point, why does every page I try to fill
bear the watermark of your sorrow?

even the winter sunset is a long pink smear

you were not that great
you were not always kind

still I cry for the waves and waves of birthdays without you
years that swell towards the shore
break in roiling sand
over my two naked feet.

Under stand

To see yourself sitting on
the bottom of the world
Everyone above you, brighter and better
to see yourself alone
no-one's ever been like this
no-one stands beside you
the reverse balloon of your ego, a black prick
sucks everything in then
disappears
it is now nothing and you are at its centre
your last word not the oath of a dropped shoe or nicked cheek
what you said and what you did were one
unity of thought and action
Shoot.

My version

Last night I spit in her face
it was the only weapon to hand
you know how hard it is to get your limbs to move in sleep
water came back at me
spittle or tears, they were the same
I knew I made a good target
when I aimed barefaced at her.
At Christmas, my husband stood in
and even though I slammed his face once, twice,
hard into the dancehall table
I got no relief.
A couple of years ago I pushed my therapist off the piano
bench with my hips, in mid-duet
this was my mother too
then I had to play alone.

Sometimes I feel so darn catty

Diana, tall white cat across the street
sits on her porch
paws immaculate
yes, pressed together in front of her chest
over here, I'm listening to Largo from Xerxes
the old king weeps under a tree
for his kingdom or something
(the bride doesn't have a clue
when I play this for her wedding, barely *adagio*;
at her mother's funeral, I let the sorrow bleed through)
Diana, you may be sure, is not Hercules
the fat Persian down the lane
who noses big love into my hand
and anyone else's who happens along
last night I saw him (absolute whore!)
stumble up the street after a perfect stranger
Do you ever sit and do nothing?
My therapist wants to know
and I say, yes, sometimes

and until this moment, it's been a lie.

**A hooker flashes her breasts on Jarvis as
we drive home from the poetry workshop**

And those breasts of hers are timeless
two touching odes
the wellspring of all first nourishment

Where is the reader, I wonder,
to slow down and stare at our poems
the ones we slaved over tonight
to cup them in lusty hands
just to feel their weight
or run a finger down the page
and watch those stanzas dance?

All evening we've crammed our lines into girdles and bras
snapped shut with periods and other full stops.
Made a dress of the whole nine yards
argued over the blue coat versus the green coat
the orange coat versus the red coat
or no coat at all

On Jarvis, we tailors in the car are toiling still
what about a flowered coat
no-one mentioned flowers
I'm thinking flowered could work:
we shall have clothes for the Emperor sometime soon

And out from the sidewalk
those breasts shout their bright hello
their quick goodbye

Nature's perfect text.

Sons: drowning

The tombstone the river the farm
I have never felt their help in telling my story

Father, mad as hell, often took off his belt in company
hauled one of us out to the porch
cries soured the cabbage
tears were just desserts

Mother, soft, Bible-reader, mama cat
needlepoint
Home Sweet Home
where the heart is, always a hat on in church
Spare the Rod
these were hung in every room
Jesus' hands were kind hands
never forgetting the possessive, that bit of thread
and Spoil the Child

The night of our drowning
we bolted our supper
afraid of the dropped fork, the spilt milk
the shouts, the cries, the belt
headed for the river bend
where the water was the deepest, the fastest, the coldest
horseplay and yells
water pushing air up and out of our warm summer lungs
heaved up on the bank to rest
I was watching when he went down the first time
bearing the weight of our father's name
his second time became my first

I was compelled
I had my mother's good intentions, water-logged trunks
his third became my second
if I let him go and survive, there will be punishment
and a thousand years of mother's pursed lips
turning away towards the sink

And then we both fell silent.

Medicine Man

Dance, oh yes, he can dance, and wants to dance with me, sisters,
of these he has plenty, Violet, Goldie, so fast he sings the names,
I cannot get them down, it's no use writing, his daughters, both
twenty, not dancing now but driving, driving us through the
night, after the party, back seat of the Sky Chief, how handsome
he seems in the morning's first light, how healing those hands,
and his daughters, both driving.

Zumburger

Zumburger and you've spent two weeks trying to remember the name twenty-five years later Zumburger across from Rochdale where he shared a gnostic with two other students you can't think of their names it's not important Go to the Zumburger where you sit watching him bring two coffees down the stairs thick white mugs on a brown plastic tray he would always spill some nicotine shakes even then and other drugs, mescaline, peyote, hashish on an electric welder thin spiral of smoke sucked up through the bottom of a retractable ball point, the only one you tried But meet him in the Zumburger first, where you sit clinging to girlhood such as it is at seventeen and laughing at all his jokes and trying hard to make some of your own and hearing all that talk about Nietzsche and Ansel Adams and D. W. Griffiths, late sixties, and the Rochdale bed waiting across Bloor Street, the new cross-walk, you look and point, see, this is where I need to go But stay in the Zumburger and stare at the rich beige coffee and the bead down the side of the thick white mug jittery time you think the drugs and flowers make you peaceful you're waiting Across Bloor, sort of a built-in bed Scandinavian wood and a brown stain on the sheets because your period starts but you don't know how to say so you're so full of Nietzsche and Freud and Richie Havens and so you stay in the Zumburger a little longer the bent blond wood of the chairs and tables and stairs going up to the next level and there's sugar on the table mixing with the sweet tan line down the side of the cup and he says, ready? and you look around at the plants and pale wood and cigarettes with smoke spiraling up and you wait until you see he will ask again if you don't answer soon and you say, yes.

Her on the walkway by the Faculty Club

Lots of time to decide if it is
her and then to take
her measure
puffy face (from Valium?), hair still dyed red
hat (or not)
already I edit and don't live this

Lots of time to remember
the lack of response to my letter a few years back
to remember how just last week someone said
she was a no-show at a film workshop and I
jumped right in and said, that's totally what
she's like
unreliable and weird

Time to decide whether to say
Hi
(or not)
I'm nearly there
I'm almost *running into her*
though I'm not running and neither is
she
and then I greet
her and
she smiles and is past.

Friend ship

Dziękuję (Jen-KOO-yeh) thank-you and thank-you start my day at lunch, in the middle, Jane's Polish word for thank-you coming at me and her long explanation about the Polish cedilla *just like in Spanish* and her words meet my *tak* and *proszę* and *nie*, I am showing off, they fall into this little Friend Ship that tries to float between us on the table and sinks with its tonnage of words;

Or go back to first thing this morning, I wear my green silk suit and pearl earrings, in full shipshape and Bristol fashion, this is such a special day and he says, where's your overcoat, aren't you wearing a coat, you won't be warm enough without a coat, and I say, who are you, my mother, and there we are, stuck on the rocks;

And now to the Big Event, five o'clock, preening in the washroom before the Review launch, and I see this girl tricked out in pink pumps and a pink purse, she plops it on the counter and tells her two friends, you're welcome to anything in there, I bought it at the Gap yesterday, and I want to accept her invitation myself and grab the sunglasses or Tampax or lipstick, all this cargo brims out and upstairs at the reception the Pink Purse Girl wins third prize for her poem and she tells the MC she wants a pink flower, not a yellow one, and after I go to her and I want to say, you are a perfect minor third like a carillon concert but I can't;

So I go around the room with my list of the editorial board from 02 and finally find Helene, she is one of them, and she will be my friend forever if she can just rouse up one copy of the 02 edition and we plough through the setting sunlight to her place, not far at all, and in her bedroom at the co-op, I see the dissertation, the pizza, the underwear, quite the shipwreck, she gets me what I want and then I sail off to the nearest pay phone and call Malca, the Queen of all my friends, and say, I've got one, I found a copy for you, I'd just about given up, but here it is in my hand and she says, thank-you, thank-you. *Proszę*, I want to say, PROH-sheh.

Snow's prayer

Snowflakes
millions of us
each unique in her six-point devotion
each obedient to the Laws of Gravity

I dance, I fall, a scant five seconds
there's not the space of twenty-two days to play
what's left of music outside the Sarajevo Opera House

In the moment I'm framed by your window:

a turn and a bow
perhaps a pirouette
quiver, dip, ignite these lines for you
a winter's afternoon, briefly.

How to get the gun out of the loaf

This is the problem
because when I push in
(and the bread is warm, don't forget, just out of the oven)
it soothes my hand, I want to leave it there,
get massaged by this muffin pillow

And that is a shame
because my terrorist cell relies on me
in my work at the bakery
get the weapon out
don't get caught
one gun in every fifth loaf
sometimes in every second
you see, they never know for sure
I am not informed
only I do sense, from the daily search,
the tenderness, the grip
of the round fresh food.

Ice again

He is a gnome, a short man, a fool, but he can drive this big lumbering bus, sometimes sleek & silver, through the deep snow, he drives it up the steep hill crawling out of Neustadt & then loops around & drives up the hill again, our tracks the only ones going out of town but I am not surprised, I know we will always be alone, & we drive up the hill again & again & just when I think we are out on the highway, we are back again, tackling the hill & finally on the road to the city & now we are going too fast & the bus careens into the ditch but the gnome gets us right again & he is going so fast I shout out *slow down* & I can see trees & ravines & rocks where I will be hurt, my body feels the pain & then a bare grey patch where his speed is good but over so quickly & then there is ice again.

Pentecost

agua now an awful, dry vowel
in the mouth of my tomato-neighbour
agua every second word
puffy face: my mother looks past me out of the mirror
try to remember the last day we had rain
mind on fire
flames without words
no end in sight to the weather
eyes of a battered child stare from the bottom of *The Sun*
two weeks before his death
and red bruises from a video picture
worth a thousand
Pick up the sticky bits from the street
make a walking collage
the sky cannot give us what we need
the earth burns with fever
talk to God and surrender
let the tongues of fire rain down.

The next attack

I look for portents in the kitchen
spill the bottle, briefly, but what a mess
water everywhere, under the dishes on the counter
mop up, groan

Cut my finger, not badly, on the paring knife
slicing a cucumber
blood on flesh, blood on tissue

It gets trickier after dark
then the real estate agent knocks on the door
come in, come in, it's cold outside
her nosy Parker pen in my face, just sign this card for your new
neighbours, they're moving in tomorrow
and I uncover this slick saleswoman, to see
a body covered with thin plastic explosive
she hugs me as bombs go off
pop pop pop

And later still, in bed
you no longer trust me with your needs
I have loosed my tongue on the world, gossiped
now it will be years
until we can be that close again.

She crosses the hump-back bridge in twilight

Quickly I wrote tennis shoes in, warm and comfy
to heal her bruised feet
those dress shoes exploding into
long nails, acrylic bits and the plastic sole
so treacherous on tarmac
now she won't have to hitch a ride
in the Young Offender's Mustang
he is headed in the wrong direction anyway
but if tennis shoes appeared when needed,
why not other protection,
more than she can imagine, against more than she can fear?
Then a new crisis, the key crisis, nearer the house
she's forgotten them again
not to worry
I slip them into her jacket
and now she stands gazing at her bright-eyed home,
the kitchen set like a jewel in the front window.

Your haircut is from Africa

All the tender pink bits
you laid bare to tall men, black and angry
their tools colder than razors
while I trembled in the Embassy
inventing curfew

Now I plan to take my leave, take nothing else,
no souvenir of the danger

Won't you bend down, one last time,
let me comb some rain through your locks,
make your head a hard blond bonnet
The bland and dusty Prairies were my home
before I flew here
we can make water
go further than most
you yourself may find this skill
somewhat utile

I can spot Castro for you, at some distance,
stalking us through the trees
– my eyes were honed in a blizzard –
I know that body well
carbine, shoulder strap, ammo clip
the finest profile of any man
I've ever thought to marry
or betray.

Prehistoric

Before the time when I thought of writing it down

in a bar
I am standing drinking
at the bar
raising the shot glass to my lips
I am drinking
he is beside me
I don't know if he's drinking
I raise the glass to my mouth, drink
I am standing at the bar
he is beside me
he may or may not be drinking himself

I am in his apartment on the leather couch
leathery like an S & M mask
he tries to put his hand between my legs
I reach down to stop him
the couch is black leather
boxing gloves
and he pushes his hand between my legs
I reach down to stop him
we are on the couch
knight's leather gauntlets
leather everywhere
as he reaches down
and I stop him

I am at the top of the escalator at the station
I am dizzy, falling
I want to be quit of him
I want to get away
but I am not running
I am dizzy and falling
he has walked me to the top of the stairs
and I feel myself falling
without conversation or soundtrack
he is watching and I am about to fall

before there were words to write it down.

Sunset Bar & Grill

I've grown old waiting for you
in the Sunset Bar & Grill
hunched over my whiskey, feet
hooked on the barstool rungs
memory dog off in the distance barks
speak up, speak up, speak up
long time since I've had
two words
to rub together
got something going, friction
    maybe a fire
useless

once I sensed you coming through the door
when you saw the set of my shoulders
you probably figured I'd given up
I was no longer expecting
so in the time it took me to jump down
twist around, look
you disappeared
saw one pant leg, that's all
so many conclusions, so little evidence
your love itself, I'd have to include in that sweeping line

every night, at last call
the bartender drags his rag through gin tears and change
That's the story, Morning Glory
as if I'd scribbled out a final paragraph
satisfied with the ending
after all.

Losing the poetry contest

I am Robert E. Lee
the pacifist who didn't want to fight
but felt obliged
Time, Circumstance, Victorian values

First it's my proud stallion
on his painful back, in the river bed
tries to get up
I have to look away

This is where my husband says,
it's just a movie
or in this case, just a contest
helps me shield my eyes

But it's not *just a contest*
for now I stand with my two lieutenants
in the stream
handsome in our Confederate cloaks
beautiful pearl, never was grey so vibrant
our flower child hair glints silver,
gathered at the nape
and faces calm with the Peace
that still deserves a chance

The little Yankee leader
waves a paper sword

I claim this land for the Yew Ess of Eh, he pipes
as if they will own the Mississippi
flowing on, through our tall, stately bodies.

Comfort, Swan, Gentles

Names more than names
what his was, I've totally forgot
or really, never knew
that's the truth of it

It was September
it was College
it was the Sixties
we were anxious and Wilde
we wore Peace (Pease?) on chains

              his

unknown   ☮   student

              mark

Was he a sign at the stock market
a hand cupped to the ear
Shell or Schelle or Schell?

Two million people in the phonebook on my lap
flimsy names on pages
but the good news, with all these crowds
No More Lonely Nights!

Was he a colour – Scarlett, Gold – or even, Greene?

PANE – see also Payne, Pain, Paine
no, that's not it

Was he a city – Paris, London, Washington?

Yu Wunder Howe
this curiosity happens
every Childe, Boye and Mann
can make sense
thrown together with a bit of Art

Tse what I mean?

Music, a food for love

Thank-you for the Streetcar Serenade –
Merle Haggard and Hank Williams
were just what I needed last night
Who wrote the Book of Love, is what I want to know

You got off too soon
a common flaw in musicians
If there were such a thing, my hand
would have snaked up the window
to pull the *Don't Stop* bell

You went underground, I stayed on,
to rock through the runny neon of Chinatown East
then warm myself on the skyline's red ashes,
now at some distance

It's dark
It's almost Christmas
my turn to get off
a candy bar should see me home
"Cold and damp out there,"
I tell the candy bar clerk
who bundles yesterday's news
"Right, that'll be $1.10," he says,
as if comments on weather now have a price

Take it and run

Out on the street, forego the umbrella
to manoeuvre the chocolate
Come on, rain,

wet my head, bare hands, wrapper

And now another miracle manifests
in this Season of Wonders

How the caramel, once hot and bubbly,
got smoothed into each firm brown square.

Room for love

They're tearing down the dorm
across from where I sell my poems
trouble with this campus now
there's no room for love
once there was love, love just everywhere
love in the sine, love in the cosine
in the equation
love in the logos
love for the numbers, love on your arm
love in the tattoo
even love in Amsterdam, over the summer
love along Bloor Street
it danced with Hendrix, it cried with Joplin
under the carillon
after the Eucharist
love in the French verbs
love in our *je t'aime*
love late on Tuesdays
love in the stadium
love ran in sneakers
into the dry cleaners
love at the Embassy
love in the tennis court, love in our omelette
everywhere, everywhere
room for love.

Art: he paints my portrait with gifts

The first year:
an iron lantern held a pale candle
a spark, a flame, this was our new passion
he said I tasted of peaches
when he kissed
the land of my buttocks
the great plains of my thighs
a tropical country his tongue travelled to
again
again
and again

The next year:
lavender from his healing garden
the greatest pleasure, he said
to be a man who loved a woman who loved a woman
lavender for his faithfulness
while I spent the odd weekend in other arms

The third year:
an earthenware teapot
memento mori, I believed at first
to dust you will return
but when its empty cavern filled with tea, hot and good
tea steeped for hours in my pot-bellied mind
when I poured it out to strangers at four o'clock
I saw it was my cooking pot
my casserole of drafts

The last year: cherubim
my friends said,
a reproach for the children you never gave him
but I see the cherubim swelling into seraphim
birth-messengers who will seek me out, some day soon
I will not laugh in their face
nor ask, how can this be?
No, I will be quick to bear what they bring
go ahead, pen your sentences on my body
ecce ancilla domini

Overcoats: hers and hers

My mother
a stone
who wanted me for a mountain

We sit in overcoats
she asks how I feel, about her dying
nothing is what I feel
but where to hide?

First I blame her coat
she must take it off
set an example
show me what's inside

When she doesn't budge
I get up and set our table
with platitudes, knives

"I can't believe…"
"Remember the time…"
"You know, Dad never really…"

Ah, *ma petite chou!*
You hoped to grow an elm when you had me
but too soon used, too much bent
down from heights that we forgot
we both were reaching for.

That night, my first song

Listen, he said, that woman crossing the street
you can hear her high heels on the pavement

me in his arms, sixteen floors up

the sheets he put on the bed
warm from just out of the dryer
feel them, he said
before we made love

window barely open
wind through late October trees
some rustling left
and the woman walking, sixteen floors down

those raw melodies
before I put them to words
before the pie charts of middle age
what percentage of couples say 'I love you'
once a month or less
what percentage, never.

Artist's basement

Sorry about the stairs. Watch your step. The landlord's always promising a light and new treads. Yeah, right!
Here we are. Might just as well start with this one.

I

Driver napping on a park bench while his passengers wait on the curb. One breaks rank to walk towards the railway underpass off in the distance
Definitely an east-end painting. The railway pass is a dead giveaway. Somebody once complained, the guys in your paintings are always asleep. You know something? He's right.

Here's an interesting one.

II

Sunlight through grimy Plexiglas onto multi-coloured Japanese parasols; one diner below in the restaurant
Bit of a departure for me, really. Doesn't take long for a style to paint you into the proverbial corner. I say, so what!
Nice contrast, though, all those umbrellas and then one plate, one knife, one fork, well, you get the picture.

III

This one, well, that's certainly Post-coital Languor, that's what I should call it. Had a lot of trouble with the face. Once I start socializing with my models, only the torso comes out looking human, the rest is just, I don't know, abstract.

IV

Le Baiser
A kiss, but ambivalent, as if it's a sibling and you shouldn't. A French title can hide a multitude of sins.
Again, not much of a face on anybody. You know, I read somewhere that Hitler didn't get into Art School because he couldn't paint heads. Now that's scary!

V

This one I like to call *Accident* – or maybe even *Still Life with Dog*. See the bits of broken glass and just a hint of blood in the corner – sort of, like, seeping into the picture – or seeping out, you could say, depending on your point of view.
The dog? Well, that may be a tail in the other corner.
Or a nose.
Sometimes I think I've run out of ideas. I'll never paint again. People just say, do anything, paint a light bulb and a light switch. They just don't get it. That's not painting at all, that's copying down, that's rhyming off or something. Easy for poets, you just listen to those voices all day; it's automatic writing. You stand over the page and let the words drop, splat, wherever they fall, that's the poem right there. Call it *Light bulb & switch*. Paint a cage around the bulb and call it *Interrogation*. Now we're getting somewhere!

VI

A letter spasms on the tracks in the wind and the rain; a crowd looks on in horror as someone tries to grab it, oblivious of the angry red streetcar hurtling in
If I had to pick a favourite, this would be it. Why, I'm not sure. Undefined heads and hands on the human figures again. A sign of childhood abuse? You decide.

VII

When you first see this one, you might say, it's just a black wash, it's the middle of the night, where's the relaxation music and toothache I fell asleep with, but look closely, there's a little kidney bean brain-dot in the upper right. This could grow into something large and impressive. One would hope.
(nervous laughter)
Well, that's it, folks. I guess you've got a few more stops to make this evening. Hang on. I'll see you out. Those stairs are a bitch.

His sister

His sister, a beautiful woman
I met and liked and saw for lunch
to which she always came late
then she told me about being his sister
about being introduced like that

this was a surprise

Have you ever had to unpack by yourself
she would ask, out of breath
all your furniture and clothes and bedding
or
I went to the passport office on my way here and
there was such a line-up

So after the third time
which was the worst time
I mean, I was ready to order dessert
I never saw her again
but now when I see him on TV, famous, talented
I think of his sister
beautiful
always late.

Notes for a piano

Keys: harvest them from old 45s in your basement

For the wood, go deep into the forest where the partisan weeps
for his wife and children

The basses you can find in a dark green oxygen pond
aswim with tadpoles

The trebles dance on spume
in the wake of a fast red yacht

You've often seen the damper pedal
from the window of a northbound train,
fashioning its blue silence under the snow

Felt for the hammers you can get at any corner shop
where Old World men gather to smoke their cigars

The gold letters of the Maker, this is the hardest part
you will have to gather them slowly
evening by evening
from cold April sunsets on the farm.

When Dot Huffman dies

When Dot Huffman dies there will be no more coughing. Silence will fall over the church like a warm towel after a shower. People will look round their pew, not spotting the difference, and think, new carpets, the minister has shaved his moustache, maybe it's snowing outside. At the scripture, when Dot used to cough the most, they will hear the story of the woman at the well as if for the first time; when Jesus says, drink of the water I give you, and never thirst again, they'll think, what a wonder, why haven't I heard *that* before in all its quenching splendour, how the mind can wander, and there will be Dot, not coughing.

Before first kiss

A good poem is the soft moment before first kiss
anticipation
the poems looks at you, intense, ready to ask a question
or confess

A good poem might flash love in the first line
a hint, an allusion
not yet moving in the body
nor marred by the act itself

The poem leans towards you,
it wants to, badly
it asks, but not in so many words
pressing on your overcoat

Anything is possible
the colours of a black and white photo
the one they call *The Kiss*, perhaps
before the shutter closed.

I could ask

I could always ask
what the jellied beets and mixed veg mean
I mean, asking is an option
I could ask what, exactly, *they* mean
the jellied beets and mixed veg
that is, if I managed to catch him
before he ascended the stairs to his clinic
I could spot him in his white lab coat and ask
what do they mean, the vegetables and the beets

And he might say, you're late, I said 6:11
and I'd have to say, you're right, I am late, you did say 6:11

Or perhaps he'd say, what does mean, mean
you always want meaning

But I could always ask
I could ask him, eat in or take out?

I could ask, why me? Why not her, or her, or her, or even her?

And he would probably say, you're late again, you're always late

But I could ask
and see if he knows.

Resolution

This will be my year of details

Women in the theatre washroom
discuss leaky bladders
it's the cold weather that reminds
one had hers lifted and put in a sling
I've heard of that, another says
end of problem

Grandpa's last team
were horses named Bill and Fred
all the great grandkids wanted to know
when they saw the family movies

7 a.m. the young man outside Pape Station
wears red high tops
dawn just pinking the sky
already days lengthen, as my resolution holds
smokes ganja and saunters downstairs to the train
in a haze of sweet oblivion

Chekhov's at 891. in the Dewey Decimal System
(Russian literature, alphabetical)

My brother, the one who will preach in Africa
fears most Niagara Falls and snakes
in his dreams

I keep the label from the socks
(5% angora, 3% cashmere)
bought at Legs Beautiful
it says *touch me/touchez-moi.*

A lesbian and her lover in Siberia

I can be happy in any old exile
so long as you are there
cabbage soup and potatoes under fluorescent tubes

Fourteen candles on December 6
make our own private Yule
safe from the patriarchy of Christmas
no babies, no salvation

What we write, we read aloud to each other
the page is cold, but oh so straightforward.

Once, back then

This would have been around the time of

>*I can't go ahead with this*

when I thought I didn't hear what you said
when Nasser died in Egypt and you flew over with the film crew

>*I think we should pack it in*

I was just finishing my exams
Polanski had been arrested

>*We're planning on getting married, you know*

The Shah of Iran fell
a mass of confusion
that night there were four messages on my machine
one, an invitation to your sister's fortieth

>*I never said I loved you*

The Royal Wedding

I'm sweeping out the basement, finding stuff everywhere.

Workshop

The dictionary skitters across your larynx with a great racket
to land as a building crew
using saliva and wood fibre to redecorate the Men's Room
bowls of pencils and much gurgling fluid;
you will spend all of tomorrow denying this
or looking for bluebottles under the Toyota
whose great green heart beats into a giraffe
offering Brazil nuts to the soccer team
anyway, the season's darn near over.

Days of nothing

Temperature reaches zero
most days in January
the sum of its achievement

My phone call to Mom is hollow at the centre

"1,000 cookies every Christmas
10 of them get together to make a batch
some roll, some cut, one mans the oven
sorry you couldn't be here."

Could God himself and God's own Son
have nothing at the core
love gone
life blown out through the donut hole
reamed by an atheist's axiom?

And after the boo-hoos of Eunoia's o-section
did Bök not cool off
look, bootless, for boon
for meaning beyond nothing
some good in his echo
something, anything, not ending with zero?

A good poem is better than ten novels

Well, better than the ten novels I've never written anyway, age fifty-two, it's just not happening, but then you'd never get the first Sunday of Daylight Savings Time in a novel, man, that sun just won't quit, 6 p.m. and it's time to head to the Dairy Queen, I'll punch my order in as I walk over there, one large butter pecan sundae, a whisper of salt on those pecans, warm from the oven, hot sauce humming its way right through to the bottom, look at that sun, won't you, and when I sit down at the table with my prize, a toddler in a booster seat turns and yells *herro* to me, just me, *eat your ice cream before it melts, Claire*, says her mother, and *herro* she says again, boy, that sun shows no sign of stopping.

Poetry makes my living

The Paint Factory: my first job
where I named the colours
Watermelon Falls
Blueberry Smoke
those two were mine
bet you never knew that!

Then it was stand-up at Yuk Yuks
didn't last long
– excuse me if you've already heard this one –
There's this surrealist writer, see, you wind him up
and the sales pitch goes
He walks, he talks, he says dada!
Not that funny, eh?
Well, like I said, I didn't last past Christmas

Then it was piano lessons
or more specifically
new versions of mnemonics for the notes
re-doing that old chestnut "every good boy deserves favour"
so I came up with
Easter gods bring dark Fridays
and
English goofs buy Danish fritters
there was only so much of that that needed doing
so the job dried up, as it were

Then finally – and I'm still at this gig –
funeral orisons
I already had the black suit and beret
so the uniform wasn't a problem
also, quite used to begging (Canada Council and all that)
and I can put a good spin on just about any corpse
you wouldn't call it lying, exactly
at least I wouldn't
but then
it's my living, isn't it?